Highlights

The
GREAT
BIG
Book of
My First
Puzzles

HIGHLIGHTS PRESS
HONESDALE, PENNSYLVANIA

Art by Xiao Xin

Birthday Party

Every birthday party item here has one that looks just like it. Find all 10 matching pairs.

By Tanya Seale
Art by Laura Logan

Find the Flowers

Flowers, flowers on the vine,
I want to pick you,
Make you mine.
But since you don't
Belong to me,
I'll sniff you, then
I'll let you be.

Use your finger to help the girl find the purple flowers. How many butterflies do you see? What else can you count?

Sidewalk Art

Envelope

Paper Clip

Bandage

Peanut

Ladybug

Art by Jeff Crowther

Find the objects hidden in the picture!

Paintbrush

Spoon

Basketball

Broccoli

7

Art by Martha Aviles

Good Morning

How are these pictures the same?
How are they different?

Art by Jannie Ho

Delivering Packages

The mail carrier has delivered a lot of packages!

How many are **red**?
How many are **brown**?
How many are **green**?

What do you think is in the **red** package near the **green** door?

How many packages did he deliver?

What else do you see?

Art by Paula J. Becker

The Build-It Store

What silly things do you see?

Art by Greg Pizzoli

Ships Ahoy!

Every boat here has one that looks just like it. Find all 10 matching pairs.

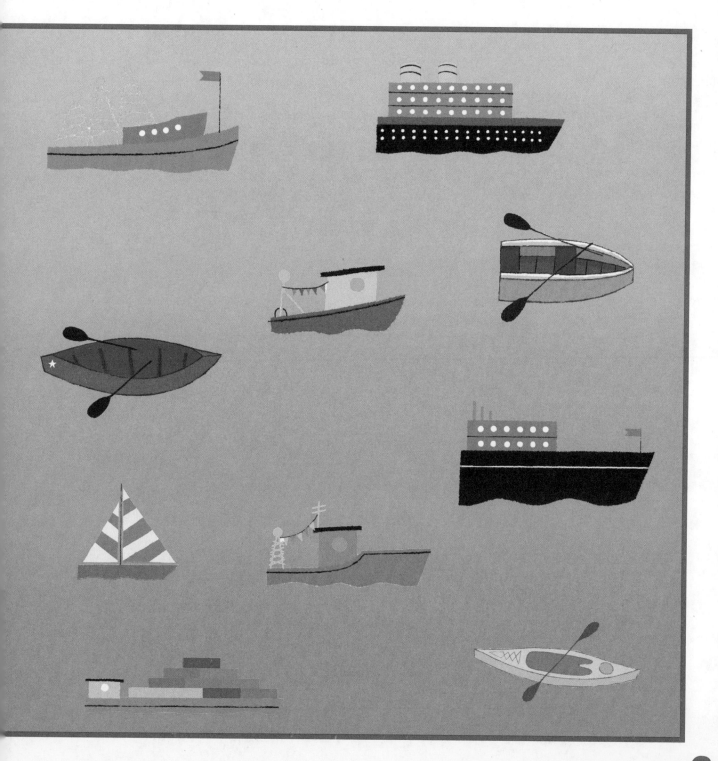

By Diane de Anda
Art by Marilee Harrald-Pilz

Guess My Riddle

I have a tail and cold, wet nose,
a furry coat from ears to toes.
I run and jump, but I'm no frog.
I'm your friend,
your fluffy _____.

I have sharp claws and soft, soft
fur, and if you pet me, I will purr.
I love to chase a mouse or rat,
and now you know that I'm a

_____.

I have long ears and a cotton tail.
I hippity-hop along the trail.
My wiggly nose is soft and funny.
I'm a cute and furry _____.

My feathers cover tail and wing.
I sit in trees, and I can sing
the sweetest song you've ever
heard. Now do you know me?
I'm a _____.

A City Hike

Ruler

Boot

Mitten

Waffle

Envelope

Art by Jeff Crowther

Find the objects hidden in the picture!

Broccoli

Fish

Crown

Crayon

Art by Julissa Mora

Fresh Produce

How are these pictures the same? How are they different?

Ants On the Go

Art by Helena Bogosian

Find the **three ants** carrying food. When they get to the kitchen, how many ants will be cooking?

Find the **four ants** carrying tools. When they get to the workshop, how many ants will be working?

Find the **two ants** wearing backpacks. When they get outside, how many ants will drive away?

What else can you count in this little ant house?

Art by Maria Neradova

The Busiest Airport

What silly things do you see?

Art by Alison Edgson

Mamas and Babies

Every mama on the left has a baby on the right. Find all 10 matching pairs.

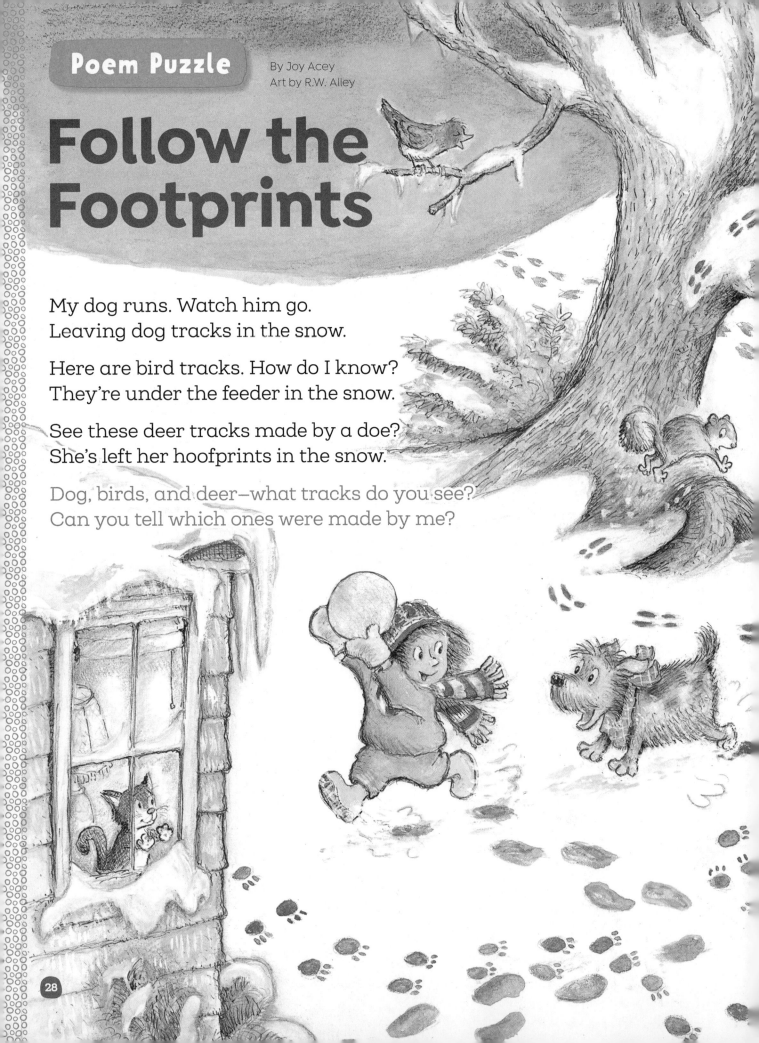

By Joy Acey
Art by R.W. Alley

Follow the Footprints

My dog runs. Watch him go.
Leaving dog tracks in the snow.

Here are bird tracks. How do I know?
They're under the feeder in the snow.

See these deer tracks made by a doe?
She's left her hoofprints in the snow.

Dog, birds, and deer—what tracks do you see?
Can you tell which ones were made by me?

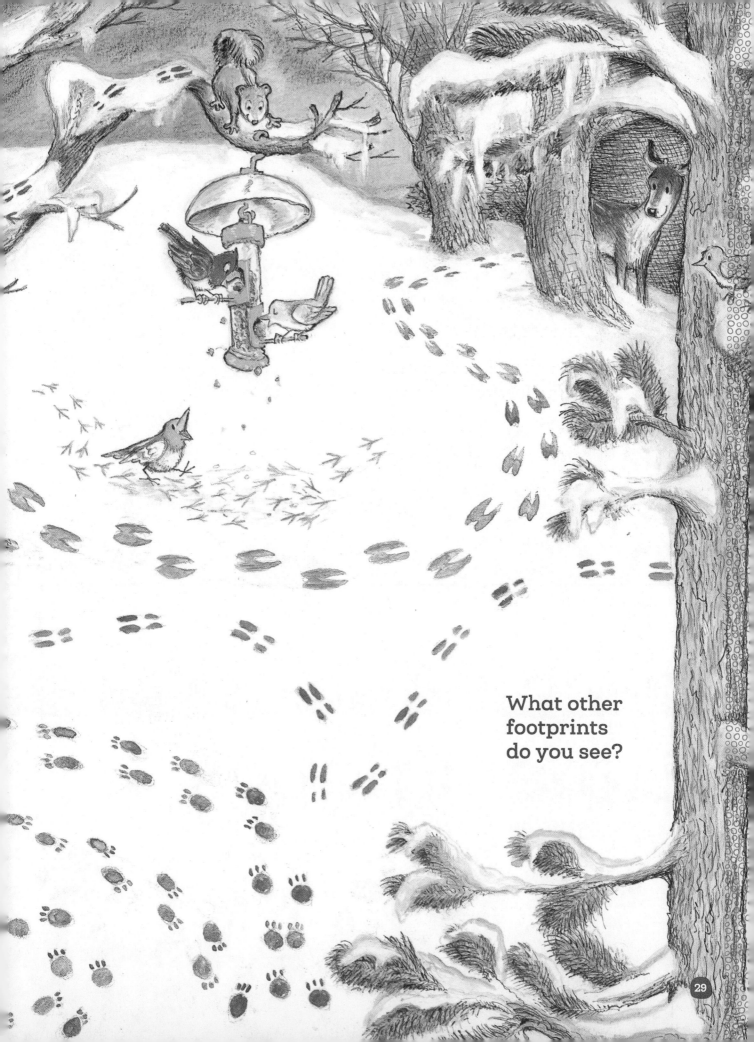

What other
footprints
do you see?

Super Friends

Pizza

Pencil

Lollipop

Almond

Broccoli

Art by Tom Knight

Find the objects hidden in the picture!

Doughnut

Kite

Envelope

Snail

Art by Martha Aviles

Board Games

How are these pictures the same?
How are they different?

Count Them

By Nancy K. Carpenter
Art by Kristin Sorra

Abacus of birds
Strung along telephone
lines.

One, two, three . . .

Count them!

What other groups
of three can you
count?

All Aboard the Train

Art by Katie McDee

What silly things do you see?

Art by Holli Conger

A Heart for You

Every heart here has one that looks just like it. Find all 10 matching pairs.

By Carrie Finison
Art by Melanie Mitchell

Find the Missing Sock

Where is my sock?

The one that is red.

It's not in my drawer.

It's not on my bed.

Mommy says, "Hurry!

We're going to be late."

Can you please help me

Find my sock's mate?

★ Where is her other red sock?

★ How many pairs of socks can you find?

★ How many socks don't have a mate?

Let's Go Fly Kites

Octopus

Alligator

Ruler

Hat

Banana

Art by Sandra Aguilar

Find the objects hidden in the picture!

Paintbrush

Book

Sheep

Button

43

Art by Linda Bleck

Keeping Cool

How are these pictures the same?
How are they different?

Art by Greg Pizzoli

Boats on the Move

How many sailboats do you see?

How many sailboats are at the dock?

How many tugboats are pulling barges?

How many fishing boats are at the dock?

What else do you see?

Art by Tim Wesson

A Carnival Adventure

What silly things do you see?

Art by Colin Jack

Say Cheese!

Every monster here has one that looks just like it. Find all 10 matching pairs.

By Sharon Hart Addy
Art by Tammie Lyon

Who's Wearing What

Zoey loves her bright blue dots.

Simon is wearing checks, not spots.

Flora likes a yellow flower.

Gary claims red stripes have power.

Lenny likes his plaid the best.
It has more colors than the rest.

★ Can you find **Zoey**, **Simon**, **Flora**, **Gary**, and **Lenny** in the big picture?

★ Which of these names have **four** letters?

★ Which of these names have **five** letters?

★ How many letters are in your name?

cabbage

tomato

beets

squash

Bunny Garden

 Open Book

 Fish

 Ruler

 Pizza

 Ice Pop

Art by Tamara Petrosino

Find the objects hidden in the picture!

Pencil

Egg

Toothbrush

Shell

Art by Jannie Ho

Time for a Trip

How are these pictures the same?
How are they different?

Art by Liisa Chauncy Guida

What Do You Think?

What's happening here?

What do you think the mother will do next?

What do you think this little guy will do after breakfast?

Do you think he'll fly his kite?

Why or why not?

His busy day is almost over.

What do you think will happen next?

Art by Katie McDee

Going Camping

What silly things do you see?

Art by Sharon Vargo

Sock Hunt

Every sock here has one that looks just like it. Find all 10 matching pairs.

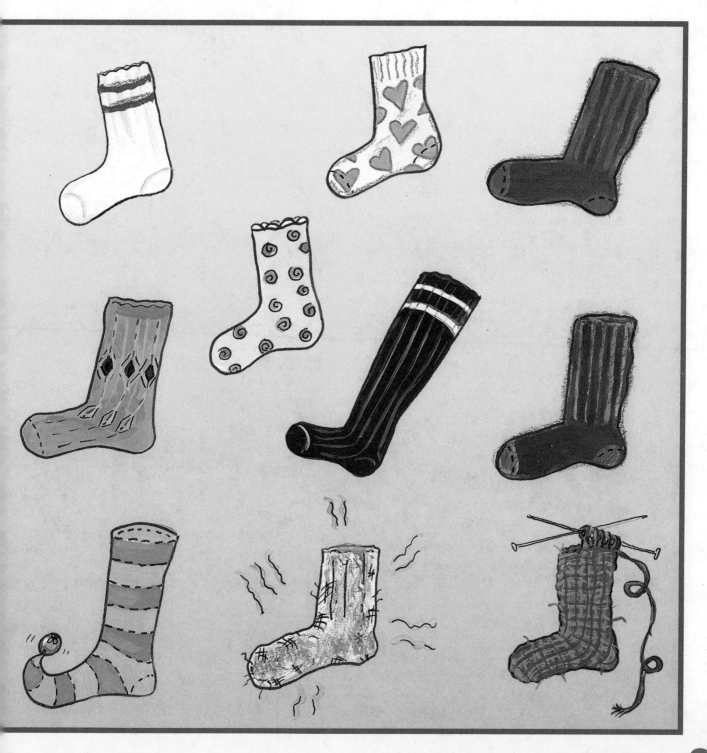

Look Out the Window

Look out the window.
What do you see?

Three pretty robins
singing in a tree.

Find all **three robins**.

What else can
you count?

By Marilyn Kratz
Art by Erika LeBarre

Time for a Trim

Bread

Crayon

Spool of Thread

Apple

Flower

Art by Amy Wilcox

Find the objects hidden in the picture!

Funnel

Slice of
Watermelon

Snail

Ball

Art by Tracy Bishop

Let's Get Wet!

How are these pictures the same?
How are they different?

Grandma Mouse's Party

Art by Olga Cheney

Benjamin Mouse wants to take some seeds, a jar of jam, and some cheese to Grandma Mouse. Use your finger to show where he must go.

★ How many **butterflies** do you see?

★ How many **flowers** do you see?

★ How many flowers have **five petals**?

★ How many flowers have **six petals**?

★ What else do you see?

Art by James Loram

At the Dog Park

What silly things do you see?

Art by Jennifer A. Bell

Ready for School

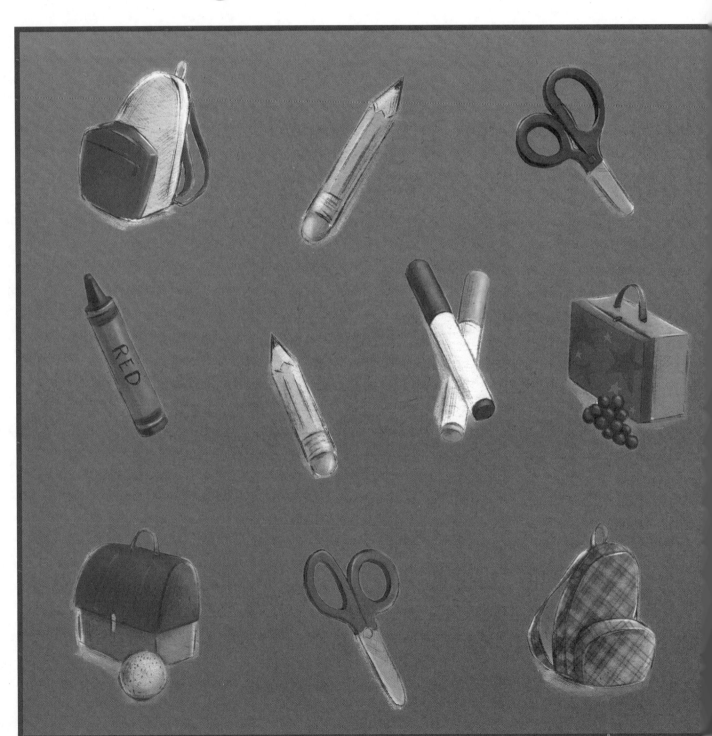

Every school supply here has one that looks just like it. Find all 10 matching pairs.

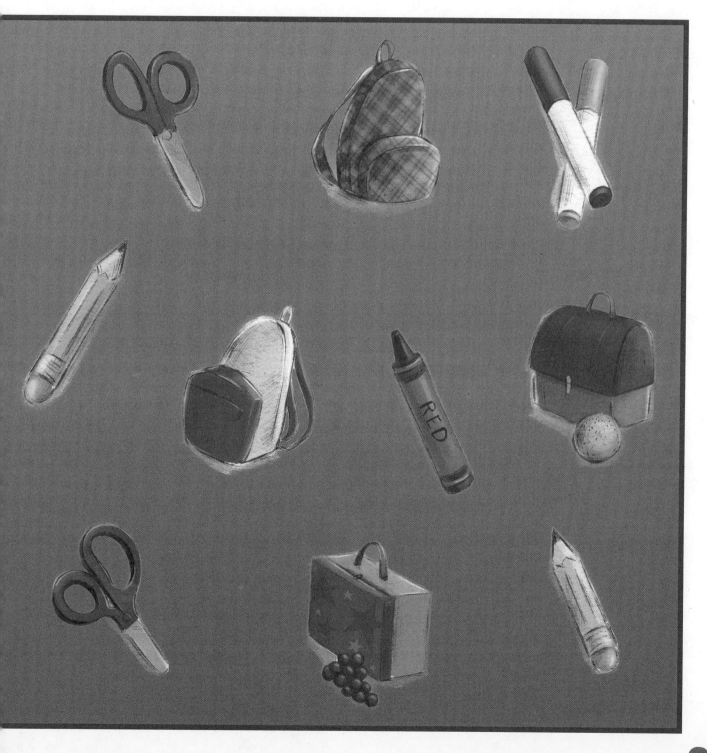

By Patricia J. Murphy
Art by Maria Maddocks

High Five

Raise a hand,
Raise it high,
Spread your fingers,
Tap high five!

Give it high...

Give it low...

Give it
everywhere you go!

From your pinkies
To your thumbs,
Let your fingers
Have some fun.

With high fives
You can say,
Hi!
Hello!
Hip, hip, hooray!

There are five candles
on the cake.

What other groups
of five can you find?

Flower Shop

Book

Toothbrush

Crayon

Lollipop

Heart

Art by Rob McClurkan

Find the objects hidden in the picture!

Rolling Pin

Envelope

Pizza

Basketball

Art by Mar Ferro

Play Ball!

How are these pictures the same?
How are they different?

Art by Jannie Ho

I spy, with my little eye, something yellow.

I Spy with My Little Eye

What do you think Dad sees?

What do you think Kelley sees?

What do you spy with your little eye?

Art by Paula J. Becker

Time to Splash

What silly things do you see?

Art by Jo Moon

On the Go

Every vehicle here has one that looks just like it. Find all 10 matching pairs.

By Sharon Hart Addy
Art by Katie McDee

Beach Feet

Lindy's wearing water shoes.

Mary Jean has sandals.

Shane is splashing in his fins.

And those bare feet are
Randall's.

Find each child named in the poem.

What kind of shoes are the grown-ups wearing?

What else do you see?

Miniature Golf

Waffle

Toothbrush

Pizza

Pencil

Crown

Art by Tamara Petrosino

Find the objects hidden in the picture!

Banana   Ruler   Sailboat   Bat

Art by Constanza Basaluzzo

On a Rainy Day

How are these pictures the same?
How are they different?

Art by Susan Swan

Counting Kites

How many kites have **stripes**?

How many kites are shaped like a **heart**?

How many kites
have **red flowers**?

How many kites
do you see?

At the Petting Zoo

What silly things do you see?

Art by Amanda Harvey

Cuddly Cats

Every cat portrait here has one that looks just like it. Find all 10 matching pairs.

By Marguerite Chase McCue
Art by Chuck Dillon

Bird's-Eye View

Up on the balcony,
Bird's-eye view.

See the rooftops,
Chimneys, too.

Up on the balcony,
Look way down.

Cars like toys
Rush all over town.

**What do you see
that's up high?**

**What do you see
that's down low?**

Time for a Carnival

Ruler

Heart

Muffin

Banana

Find the objects hidden in the picture!

Cane

Button

Pizza

Comb

Golf Club

103

Art by Kristin Sorra

Snow Day

How are these pictures the same?
How are they different?

Art by Francesca Assirelli

What's Big? What's Small?

Which window is the **biggest**?
Which window is the **smallest**?
Which critter is the **biggest**?
Which critter is the **smallest**?
Which bowl is the **biggest**?
Which bowl is the **smallest**?

What else is big?

What else is small?

Art by Carol Herring

Flea Market Fun

What silly things do you see?

Art by Rose Mary Berlin

Let's Have a Picnic

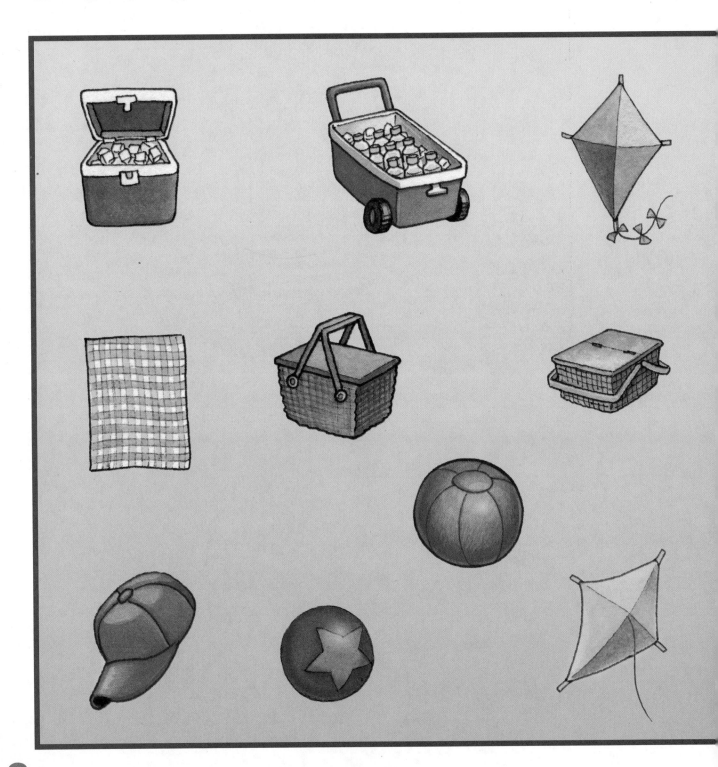

Every picnic item here has one that looks just like it. Find all 10 matching pairs.

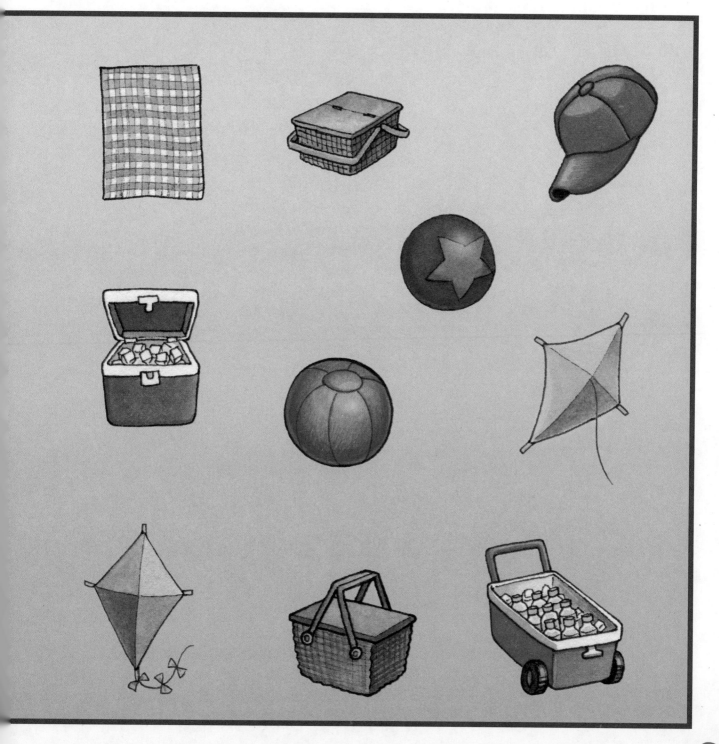

By Brite Templeton
Art by Jan Bryan-Hunt

Matching Pumpkins

Look at all the pumpkins in the pumpkin patch.

See if you can find all the pairs that match.

I think there must be more than ninety-nine.

But my favorite pumpkin is the one that's mine.

Find the eight pairs of matching pumpkins in this corner of the pumpkin patch.

What else do you see?

Under the Sea

Banana

Doughnut

Paintbrush

Crown

Balloon

Art by Patrick Girouard

Find the objects hidden in the picture!

Trowel   Glove   Ruler   Tomato

Art by Patrick Girouard

Story Time

How are these pictures the same?
How are they different?

Art by Mary Hall

Hunt for Shapes

How many rectangles can you find?
Rectangles have two long, straight sides
and two short, straight sides.

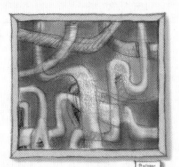

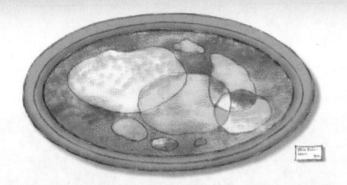

How many squares
can you find?

All four sides of a
square are the
same length.

A Fireworks Show

What silly things do you see?

Art by Greg Pizzoli

Get Moving

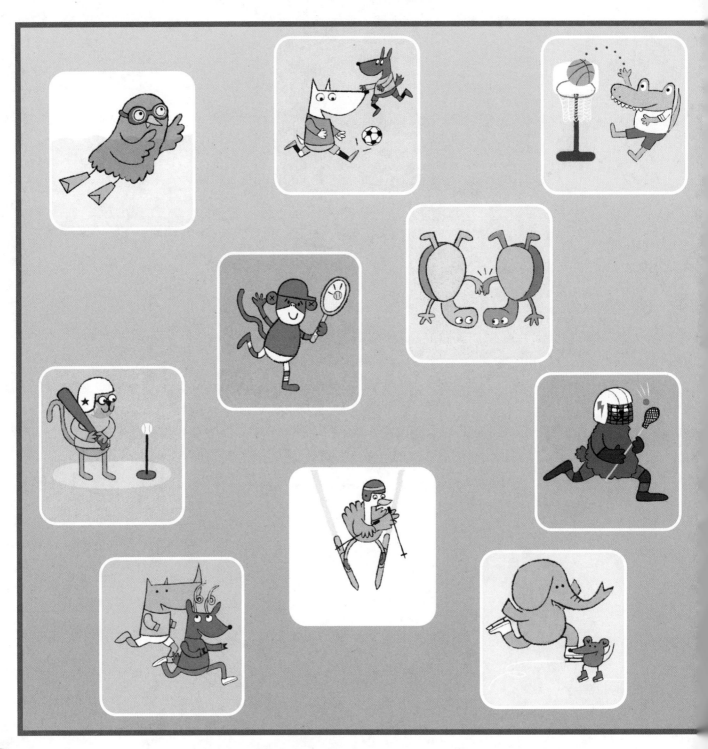

Every animal and animal team
here has one that looks just like it.
Find all 10 matching pairs.

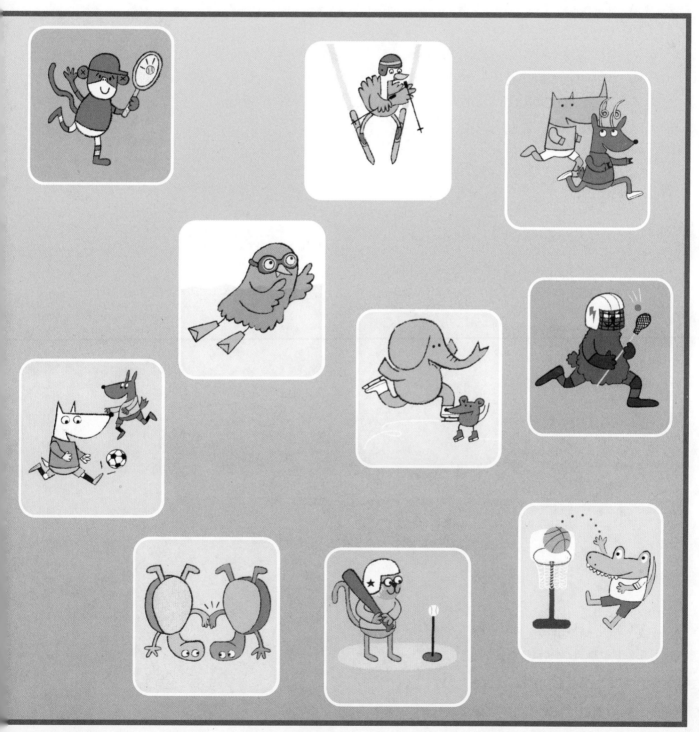

By Jan Fields
Art by Jo Brown

Dandelions

Four dandelions, bright as the sun.
Gather a handful, one by one.
Give one to the bunny.
Give one to the bee.
Give one to Mommy.
Keep one for me.

With your finger, show which path the child should take to give a dandelion to the bunny, the bee, and her mother.

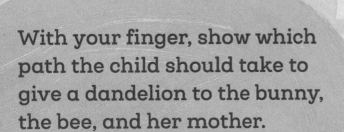

Backyard Splash

Turtle

Butterfly

Broccoli

Fish

Boot

Art by Sandra Aguilar

Find the objects hidden in the picture!

Brush

Frog

Bird

Jellyfish

Art by Susan Miller

Let's Ride

How are these pictures the same?
How are they different?

Count to Find Out

Which snowman has the **most buttons**?

Which snowmen have the **same number of buttons**?

Which snowman has the **fewest buttons**?

Which mitten has the **most stripes**?

Which mittens have the **same number of stripes**?

Which mitten has the **fewest stripes**?

Which hat has the **most spots**?

Which hats have the **same number of spots**?

Which hat has the **fewest spots**?

Art by Paula J. Becker

Getting Ready for School

What silly things do you see?

Art by David Coulson

Traffic Jam

Every vehicle here has one that looks just like it. Find all 10 matching pairs.

By Jessica Potter Broderick
Art by Anne-Julie Aubry

The Balloon Tree

If I had a balloon tree,

Do you know what I'd do?

I'd pick a yellow one for me,

An orange one for you.

And if they popped, the way they do,

I'd climb right up that tree

And pick a ruby one for you,

A purple one for me.

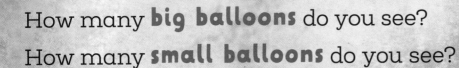

How many **big balloons** do you see?

How many **small balloons** do you see?

Which balloon would you pick?

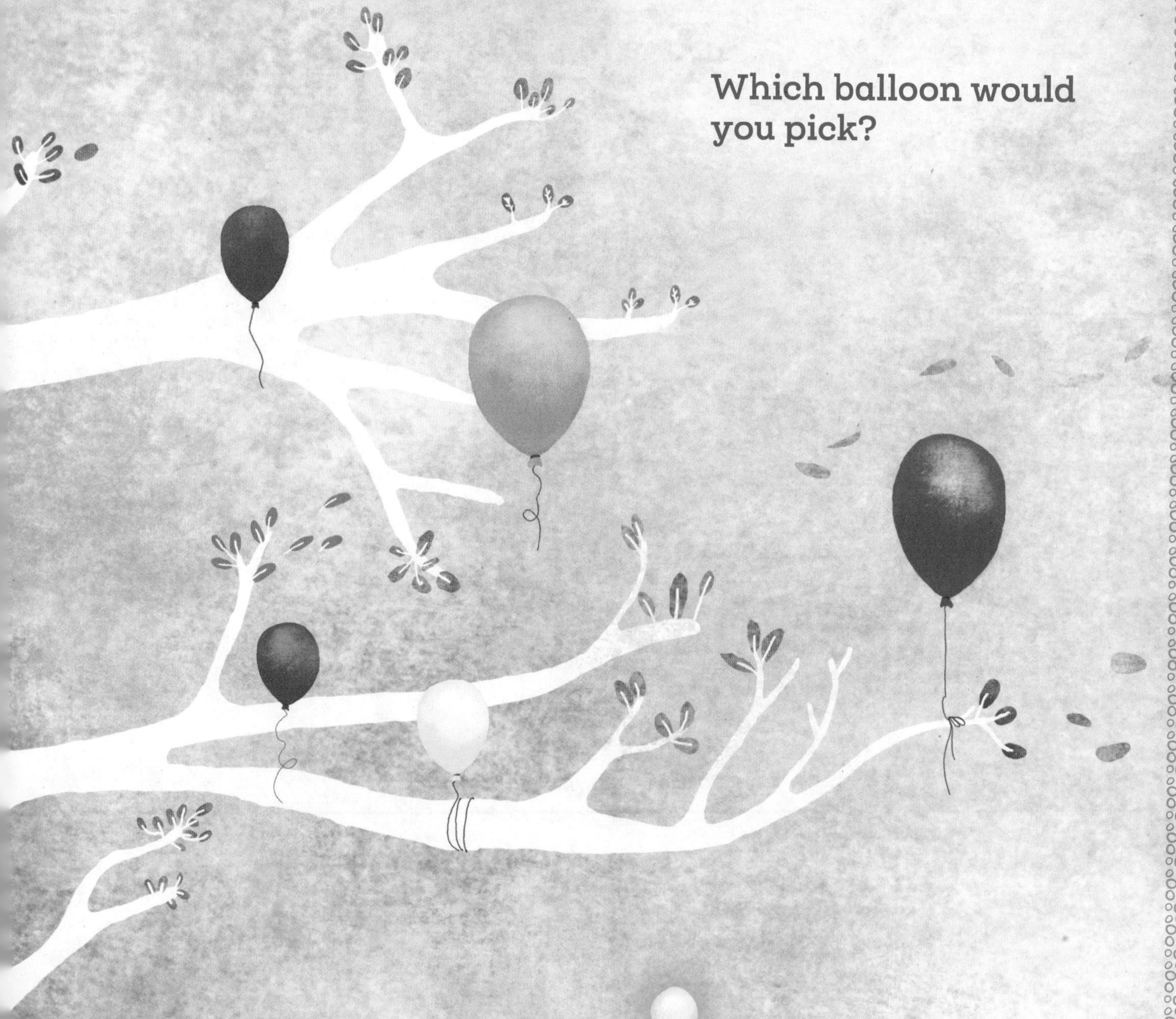

How many do you see?

How many do you see?

How many do you see?

How many do you see?

Let's Celebrate

Banana

Pizza

Bat

Ring

Ruler

Art by Jannie Ho

Find the objects hidden in the picture!

Bell

Fish

Pencil

Mitten

Art by Pat N. Lewis

Karate Class

How are these pictures the same?
How are they different?

At the Airport

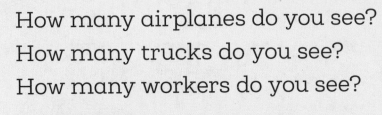

How many airplanes do you see?
How many trucks do you see?
How many workers do you see?

GATE 2A

What else do you see?

142

Art by Mike Dammer

Out and About

What silly things do you see?

Art by Dan Andreasen

Fish Friends

Every fish here has one that looks just like it. Find all 10 matching pairs.

By Charlotte Gunnufson
Art by Maggie Smith

Follow the Tracks

Tracks! Tracks! In the snow.

Let's see where they go.

In a ring around the tree,

Through the bushes, one, two, three.

To the mailbox, past the pine,

In a zany, zigzag line.

Between the swings, right by the slide,

They found the perfect place to hide.

A little hole beneath the shed,

A comfy, cozy rabbit bed.

How many rabbits are looking for a place to hide?

Do you think some rabbits are already in the comfy, cozy bed?

How many might be there?

What else do you see?

Splash Time

Crown

Muffin

Envelope

Glasses

Fish

Art by Esther Hernando

Find the objects hidden in the picture!

Ruler

Bread

Banana

Bat

Art by Paige Billin-Frye

On the Track

How are these pictures the same?
How are they different?

Art by Nancy Cote

Put Them Together

Three little spiders ran up a tree.
Two little spiders will run up, too.
How many spiders will be in the tree?

Five fat frogs are in the pond. **One** fat frog is jumping in.
How many frogs will be in the pond?

Two furry rabbits are jumping over.
Look out! **Two** more are going under!
How many rabbits will be in the garden?

Two little lambs are sleeping in the barn.
Four lambs are going in.
How many lambs will be in the barn?

Seven busy bees are buzzing round the flowers.
Look! **Three** more are coming.
When they arrive, how many bees will there be?

Art by Carol Herring

Outdoor Movie Time!

What silly things do you see?

Art by Jennifer E. Morris

Loose Leaves

Every leaf here has one that looks just like it. Find all 10 matching pairs.

By Dale Cross Purvis
Art by Jennifer E. Morris

Six Buttons

I have six buttons on my coat–
two on my pockets,
two at my throat,
two down the front
to keep me in,
far away from
the winter wind!

How many sets of **six** can you find in this picture?

Down by the Lake

Glove

Pencil

Cane

Cupcake

Broccoli

My First Hidden Pictures

Art by Betania Zacarias

Find the objects hidden in the picture!

Comb

Banana

Envelope

Football

Art by Liz Goulet Dubois

What's Cooking

How are these pictures the same?
How are they different?

Window Shopping

Art by Mike Dammer

Find the **biggest bird**.
Find the **smallest book**.
Find the **longest loaf of bread**.
Find the **shortest person**.

What else is big?

What else is small?

Construction Zone

What silly things do you see?

Art by Constanza Basaluzzo

Pack Your Bags

Every piece of clothing here has one that looks just like it. Find all 10 matching pairs.

By Mandy C. Yates
Art by R.W. Alley

Sweet Treats

One day . . .
Jack and Jill went up a hill and
Max and Spence jumped over a fence and
Kim and Lee climbed out of a tree and
Sam and Pete ran up the street.
But where was everyone going?

Who might be the
first to arrive?

Who might be the last?

A Family Meal

Lemon

Oven Mitt

Heart

Branch

Pencil

Art by Sarah Hoyle

Find the objects hidden in the picture!

Sailboat

Ruler

Banana

Pineapple

Art by Jackie Urbanovic

Watch Us Go

How are these pictures the same?
How are they different?

Art by Roberta Angaramo

How Many Puppies?

How many do you see?

How many do you see?

How many  do you see?

How many do you see?

How many puppies are in the playroom?

What else do you see?

What Busy Roads!

What silly things do you see?

Art by Sharon Lane-Holm

Mitten Mix Up

Every mitten here has one that looks just like it. Find all 10 matching pairs.

By Sharon Landeen
Art by Susan Lawson

Who Am I?

I like to eat hay
and barley, too.
When it's milking time,
you'll hear me *MOOO*.

Who am I?

In my white woolly suit,
I jump and play.
BAAAA
is the only word I say.

Who am I?

I'll give you a ride
if you get on my back.
A carrot is
my favorite snack.

Who am I?

I'm covered with feathers
and have two legs.
When you look in my nest,
you may find an egg.

Who am I?

**Now try making your
own animal riddles.**

Art with Friends

Leaf

Candle

Needle

Fried Egg

Football

Art by Paula J. Becker

Find the objects hidden in the picture!

Heart

Ring

Crown

Vase

187

Art by Dave Clegg

Delicious Dinner

How are these pictures the same?
How are they different?

Art by Katie Kath

Most and Least

Which pair of boots has the **most dots**?

Which puddle has the **most water**?

Which puddle has the **least water**?

Which umbrella has the **fewest stripes**?

Are there more kids or
more birds in this park?
How do you know?

What else do you see?

At the Train Station

What silly things do you see?

Art by Claudine Gévry

Cute Critters

Every insect here has one that looks just like it. Find all 10 matching pairs.

By Dale Cross Purvis
Art by Pete Whitehead

Hold On Tight

Snuggle up! It's warm inside.
Mama will take you for a ride.
There's lots to see. There's lots to do.
Hold on tight, little kangaroo!

As the mother kangaroo and her
joey hop along,
they see a koala,

a cockatoo,

and a duckbill platypus.

Do you see them, too?
What else do you see?

We Love Hearts

Crown

Toast

Hedgehog

Telescope

Fork

Art by Peter Francis

Find the objects hidden in the picture!

Carrot

Flower

Banana

Starfish

Art by Mary Sullivan

Let's Go Camping

How are these pictures the same?
How are they different?

Art by Erika LeBarre

Look at all These Presents

* How many presents have **striped paper**?
* How many have **polka-dotted paper**?
* How many have **plaid paper**?
* How many have **bows**?
* How many **presents** do you see?

Art by Julissa Mora

Snow On the Farm

What silly things do you see?

Art by Dave Joly

Happy Birthday!

Every piece of cake here has one that looks just like it. Find all 10 matching pairs.

Treats

Apples are crispy.
Apples are sweet.
Give me an apple,
Please, for my treat.

Apples are just
The right size to hold.
I like them best
Crunchy and cold.

By Myrna Foster
Art by Alex Paterson

How many green apples do you see?

How many red apples do you see?

What else do you see?

209

Home Haircut

Button

Pencil

Pizza

Bell

Bat

Art by Richard Watson

Find the objects hidden in the picture!

Fish

Broccoli

Snail

Ruler

Art by Jannie Ho

Let's Go Bowling

How are these pictures the same?
How are they different?

Thinking   Art by Mary Hall

Where Do They Belong?

Help Jacob clean up.

What should he put in each basket?

Think of another way Jacob could organize his toys.

At the Post Office

What silly things do you see?

Art by Dave Joly

Lots of Boots

Every boot here has one that looks just like it. Find all 10 matching pairs.

By Eileen R. Meyer
Art by Andy J. Smith

Fancy Feet

I have so many tiny feet,

It's hard to keep my sneakers neat.

They're piled up high,

They're stacked down low,

They're never in a nice, neat row.

I've searched my closet everywhere—

Can you please help me match each pair?

Kick It Up!

Heart

Mitten

Shell

Cane

Worm

Art by Jannie Ho

Find the objects hidden in the picture!

Boomerang

Comb

Ruler

Tack

Here They Go!

How are these pictures the same?
How are they different?

Art by Pat Schories

Hunt for Shapes

The swing is a rectangle.

How many rectangles
do you see?

The garage door is a square.

How many squares
do you see?

The sandbox seat is a triangle.

How many triangles
do you see?

The bear's eyes are circles.

How many circles
do you see?

What else do you see?

Art by Beatrice Costamagna

Shopping Frenzy

What silly things do you see?

Art by Dave Joly

Rock and Roll

Every groovy guitar here has one that looks just like it. Find all 10 matching pairs.

By Marilyn Kratz
Art by Judith Moffatt and Bill Hoffman

Color Rhymes

What color word completes each rhyme?

Robin has a very dark head,

but the feathers on his breast are _____.

Goldfinch is a happy fellow.

On his breast, he's sunny _____.

Sparrow hops around the town
in his suit of gray and _____.

Noisy Jay looks fresh and new
as if he'd just been painted _____.

Pigeon is a handsome sight
in blue and gray and sparkling _____.

Wash the Car

Cheese

Flute

Spoon

Feather

Art by Jeff Crowther

Find the objects hidden in the picture!

Horseshoe

Shell

Moon

Button

Ruler

Art by Sue King

It's a Puzzle

How are these pictures the same?
How are they different?

Art by Roz Fulcher

Which Has the Most? Which Has the Fewest?

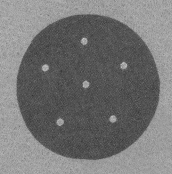

Which ball has the **most dots**?

Which ball has the **fewest dots**?

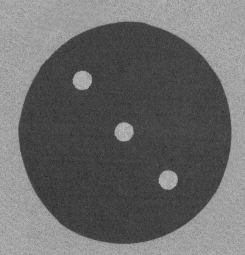

Which animal has the **most legs**?
Which animal has the **fewest legs**?

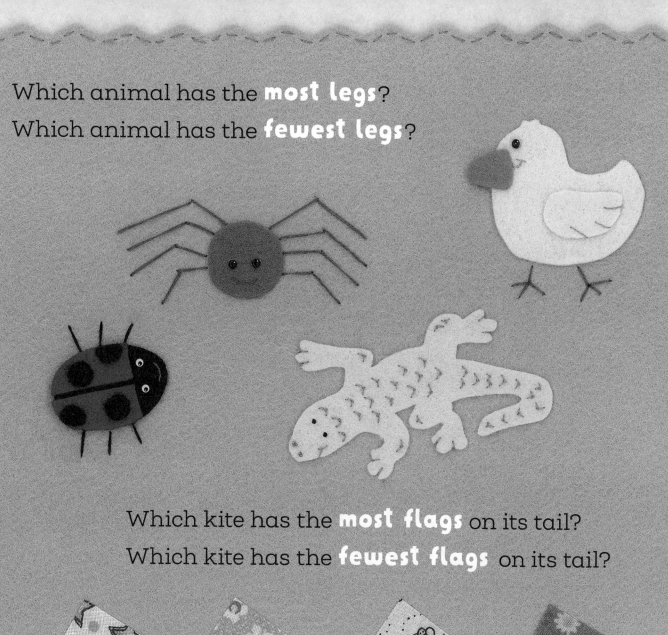

Which kite has the **most flags** on its tail?
Which kite has the **fewest flags** on its tail?

Art by Mitch Mortimer

Dino Recess

What silly things do you see?

Art by Berta Maluenda

Animal Pairs

Every animal here has one that looks just like it. Find all 10 matching pairs.

By Barbara L. Scanlan
Art by Merrill Rainey

Exploring the Ocean

Mindy's a deep-sea diver.

She's about to take a trip.

She and her cousin Dev

Made a diving ship.

"We'll explore the oceans,

Search for dolphins and blue whales,

Look for jellies and seahorses,

Find funny fish with fancy tails."

Look for the animals mentioned in the poem.

How many blue whales do you see?

What else do you see?

ANSWERS

PAGES 2-3

PAGES 4-5

We see **4** butterflies.

We also see **2** cats and **3** birds.

What else can you count?

PAGES 6-7

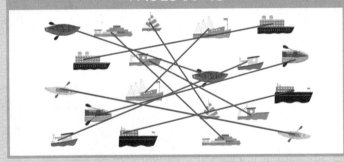

PAGES 8-9

PAGES 10-11

5 packages are red.

4 packages are brown.

3 packages are green.

We think a **scooter** is in the red package near the green door.

The mail carrier delivered **12** packages and is about to deliver **1** more.

We see **1** cat.

What else do you see?

PAGES 14-15

PAGES 16-17

I have a tail and cold, wet nose,
a furry coat from ears to toes.
I run and jump, but I'm no frog.
I'm your friend,
your fluffy **dog**.

I have sharp claws and soft,
soft fur,
and if you pet me, I will purr.
I love to chase a mouse or rat,
and now you know
that I'm a **cat**.

I have long ears
and a cotton tail.
I hippity-hop along the trail.
My wiggly nose is soft and funny.
I'm a cute and furry **bunny**.

My feathers cover tail and wing.
I sit in trees, and I can sing
the sweetest song you've
ever heard.
Now do you know me?
I'm a **bird**.

PAGES 18-19

PAGES 20-21

PAGES 22-23

5 ants will be cooking.

7 ants will be working.

6 ants will drive away.

We counted **8** toothbrushes and **8** beds.

What else can you count?

PAGES 26–27

PAGES 28–29

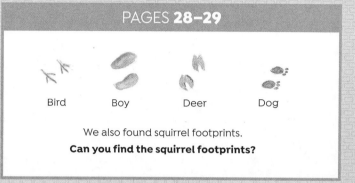

Bird Boy Deer Dog

We also found squirrel footprints.

Can you find the squirrel footprints?

PAGES 30–31

PAGES 32–33

PAGES 34–35

We found **3** telephone poles and **3** benches.

What other groups of 3 can you count?

PAGES 38–39

PAGES 40–41

There are **5** pairs of socks.

There are **3** socks without a mate.

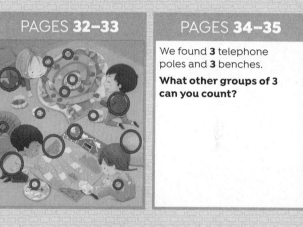

PAGES 42–43

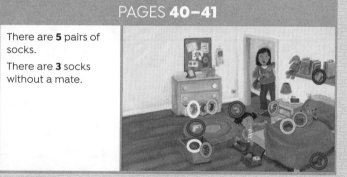

PAGES 44–45

PAGES 46–47

We see **7** sailboats. **2** are at the dock.

2 tugboats are pulling barges.

2 fishing boats are at the dock.

We also see **2** fishermen.

What else do you see?

ANSWERS

PAGES **50–51**

PAGES **52–53**

Zoey is at the bookshelf.

Simon is painting at the easel.

Flora is playing with blocks on the rug.

Gary is playing in the water.

Lenny is also playing with blocks on the rug.

2 of these names have **4** letters (Zoey and Gary).

3 of these names have **5** letters (Lenny, Flora, and Simon).

How many letters are in your name?

PAGES **54–55**

PAGES **56–57**

PAGES **62–63**

PAGES **64–65**

We also counted **3** books and **4** tulips.

What else can you count?

PAGES **66–67**

PAGES **68–69**

PAGES **70–71**

This is how we traced Benjamin Mouse's path.
Can you find another way for him to get to Grandma Mouse?

We see **7** butterflies and **3** flowers. **1** flower has **5** petals, and **2** flowers have **6** petals.
We also see **4** leaves and **1** ladybug.

What else do you see?

PAGES **74–75**

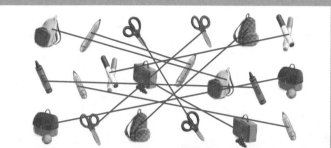

PAGES **76–77**

We found **5** presents and **5** children.

What else can you find?

PAGES **78–79**

PAGES **80–81**

PAGES **82–83**

Dad sees a yellow car, a yellow kite, a yellow coat, or a yellow cat.

Kelley sees a red car, a fire hydrant, a stop sign, a red bag, a red bird, a red dress, red curtains, or a red awning.

What do you spy?

PAGES **86–87**

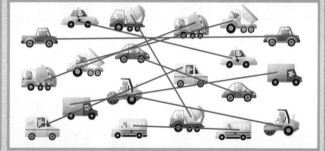

PAGES **88–89**

Lindy is on the far left with her mom.

Mary Jean is on a blanket with her mom.

Shane is in the water.

Randall is about to head into the water.

The grown-ups are wearing either flats or sandals.

We also see **3** seagulls.

What else do you see?

PAGES **90–91**

PAGES **92–93**

PAGES **94–95**

2 kites have stripes.

1 kite is shaped like a heart.

2 kites have red flowers.

We see **14** kites.

ANSWERS

PAGES 98–99

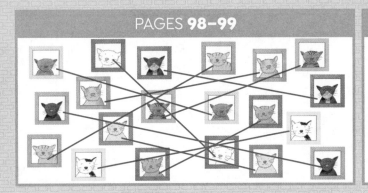

PAGES 100–101

Here is what we found. You may have found others.

Up high, we see an airplane, a helicopter, birds, a dog, and a garden.

Down low, we see cars, people, a dog, and a fountain.

What else do you see?

PAGES 102–103

PAGES 104–105

PAGES 106–107

The window in the **middle** is the biggest.

The window on the **right** is the smallest.

The **green critter** on the right is the biggest.

The **critter in the far right of the windowsill** is the smallest.

The **yellow bowl** is the biggest.

The **orange bowl** is the smallest.

The **orange chair** is also big.

The **yellow chair** is also small.

What else can you find that's big or small?

PAGES 110–111

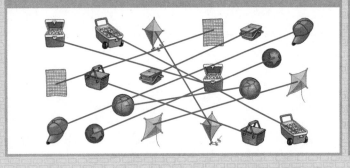

PAGES 112–113

We see a cat, a bunny rabbit, and a butterfly.

What else do you see?

PAGES 114–115

PAGES 116–117

PAGES 118–119

We found **8** rectangles and **5** squares.

How many did you find?

PAGES 122–123
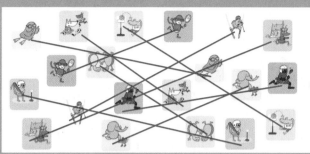

PAGES 124–125

PAGES 126–127

PAGES 128–129

PAGES 130–131

Most Buttons:
Snowman with the pink and striped hat

Same Number of Buttons:
Snowman with the red and blue hat
and the snowman with the blue and
purple hat

Fewest Buttons:
Snowman in the green and yellow hat

Most Stripes:
Orange mitten

Same Number of Stripes:
Green mitten and the red mitten

Fewest Stripes:
Blue mitten

Most Spots:
Green and yellow hat

Fewest Spots:
Red and blue hat

Same Number of Spots:
Blue and purple hat
and the pink and striped hat

PAGES 134–135
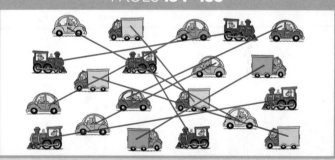

PAGES 136–137

We see **4** yellow balloons, **3** orange balloons, **2** red balloons, and **3** purple balloons.

We see **5** big balloons and **7** small balloons, including the ones that have popped.

Our favorite is the big yellow balloon.

Which balloon would you pick?

PAGES 138–139

PAGES 140–141

ANSWERS

PAGES 142–143

We see **4** airplanes, **3** trucks, and **9** workers.

We also see **8** suitcases.

What else do you see?

PAGES 146–147

PAGES 148–149

5 rabbits are looking for a place to hide.

Some rabbits might already be in the comfy, cozy bed.

What do you think?

We also see **3** birds and **1** mailbox.

What else do you see?

PAGES 150–151

PAGES 152–153

PAGES 154–155

5 spiders will be in the tree.

6 frogs will be in the pond.

4 rabbits will be in the garden.

6 lambs will be in the barn.

10 bees will be in the flowers.

PAGES 158–159

PAGES 160–161

We found **6** geese and **6** clothing hooks.

What else can you find?

PAGES 162–163

PAGES 164–165

PAGES 166–167

The **biggest bird** is red. The **smallest book** is red. The **longest loaf of bread** is next to the cakes. The **shortest person** has a red-and-white striped shirt. We see a big dog and a small dog.

What do you see?

PAGES **170–171**

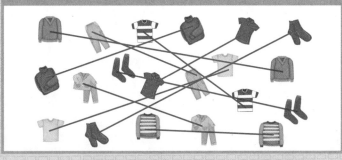

PAGES **172–173**

The boy in the red striped shirt might be the **first** to arrive. The boy in the orange shirt might be the **last**.

Who do you think will be first and last?

PAGES **174–175**

PAGES **176–177**

PAGES **178–179**

 1 There are **10** puppies in the playroom.

 3 We also see **2** stuffed rabbits.

 2 **What else do you see?**

 4

PAGES **182–183**

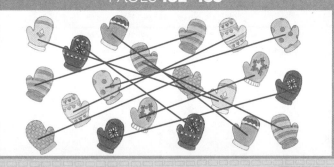

PAGES **184–185**

1. Cow
2. Sheep
3. Horse
4. Chicken

PAGES **186–187**

PAGES **188–189**

PAGES **190–191**

The **yellow boots** have the most dots.

The **puddle on the bottom left** has the most water. The **puddle below the bird bath** has the least water.

The **green umbrella** has the fewest stripes.

There are **more birds** than kids in this park. We counted **7** birds and **5** children.

We also see **3** rabbits.

What else do you see?

ANSWERS

PAGES **194–195**

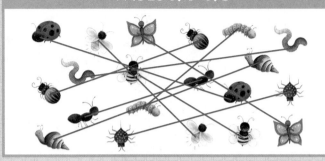

PAGES **196–197**

We also see lots of flowers.

What else do you see?

PAGES **198–199**

PAGES **200–201**

PAGES **202–203**

3 presents have striped paper.

5 have polka-dotted paper.

6 have plaid paper.

6 have bows (if you count the one the mouse is putting on).

We see **18** presents.

PAGES **206–207**

PAGES **208–209**

We see **9** green apples and **9** red apples. We also see **5** clouds.

What else do you see?

PAGES **210–211**

PAGES **212–213**

PAGES **214–215**

Jacob can put his **blue** toys in the first basket, his **green** toys in the second, his **yellow** toys in the third, and his **red** toys in the fourth.

How else can Jacob organize his toys?

PAGES **218–219**

PAGES **220–221**

PAGES **222–223**

PAGES **224–225**

PAGES **226–227**

We see **7** rectangles, **7** squares, **6** triangles, and **7** circles.

We also see a dog and a doghouse.

What else do you see?

PAGES **230–231**

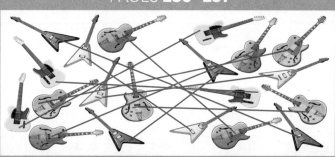

PAGES **232–233**

Robin: red
Goldfinch: yellow
Sparrow: brown
Jay: blue
Pigeon: white

PAGES **234–235**

PAGES **236–237**

PAGES **238–239**

The **white ball** has the most dots. The **dark blue ball** has the fewest dots.

The **spider** has the most legs. The **duck** has the fewest legs.

The **third kite** has the most flags on its tail. The **second kite** has the fewest flags on its tail.

ANSWERS

PAGES **242–243**

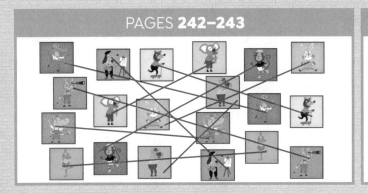

PAGES **244–245**

We found **6** blue whales.

What else do you see?

Cover art by Greg Pizzoli

Published by Highlights Press
815 Church Street
Honesdale, PA 18431
ISBN: 978-1-64472-873-4
Manufactured in Jefferson City, MO, USA
Mfg. 11/2021
First edition
Visit our website at Highlights.com.
10 9 8 7 6 5 4 3 2 1